In Grandma's Garden

Brenda West Cockerell

For
Audrey and Ella
Let it Shine !

Illustrated by Linda Ólafsdóttir

Brenda Cockerell

In memory of my friend, Holly Horton.
She will be remembered for her love of life
and her dedication to children.

I remember a time in years long past
of wonderful memories – in my mind steadfast

Of Grandma's garden – a magical place
filled with laughter and joy, enchantment and grace.

For in Grandma's garden you will see –
magic flowers 'round each tree.

She'd plant the seeds in a row
water them, weed them, watch them grow.

A stem, a leaf, a gentle shower –
each bud opens to a flower.

Her garden's enchanted, so what is your wait?
To enter, it's simple – just open the gate!

In Grandma's garden you will see –
that lady slippers waltz one, two, three

Dancing, prancing to and fro
lovely ladies in a row.

In Grandma's garden you will see –
that sunflowers shine on you and me

Shining brightly, all aglow –
casting shadows high and low.

 In Grandma's garden you will see –
cattails wave to you and me

Furry felines never sleep –
waving warnings of waters deep!

In Grandma's garden you will see –
oh my – baby's breath, so sweet is he

Softly cooing in his bed
as he nods his sleepy head.

In Grandma's garden you will see –
snapdragons snapping wild and free

Snipping, snapping everywhere –
they might give you quite a scare!

In Grandma's garden you will see –
buttercups warmed in time for tea

Melting gold, they seem to boast,
"We're creamy butter for your toast."

In Grandma's garden you will see –
foxgloves fencing merrily

Handsome devils, oh so sly –
smell their blossoms, don't be shy!

In Grandma's garden you will see –
tulips for kissing you and me

Blowing kisses in the air –
kisses landing everywhere!

In Grandma's garden you will see –
Queen Anne's lace – so pretty is she

It royally dresses her lovely sleeve.
It's regal and delicate, I believe!

In Grandma's garden you will see –
bachelor buttons – one, two, three

Bright and shiny to look his best –
a dapper row adorns his vest.

In Grandma's garden you will see –
a dandelion waiting 'neath a tree

He's a furry, fussy gent.
Oops! the wind – guess where he went.

In Grandma's garden you will see –
a tiger lily hunting you and me

She's here, she's there, you feel her stare –
But, it's all in fun, her stripes declare!

But, once a year so magically, in Grandma's garden you will see –
a hollyhock for you and me.

She seems to laugh and smile from high –
her berried blossoms grace the sky!

The light grows dim and shadows creep –
time is late, it's time to sleep.

Pause at the gate – draw memories near
with laughter and joy, peace and good cheer!

In Grandma's garden take a peek
It's so much fun – play hide and seek!
Look here, look there to play the game,
see how many you can name.

snails	mice	holly
butterflies	shoes	sun
ladybugs	lions	mailbox
bees	tigers	gate
dragonflies	babies	foxes
fish	dragons	lips
birds	teacups	kisses
cats	teapots	hearts
dogs	buttons	weathervane
crowns	Grandma	moon

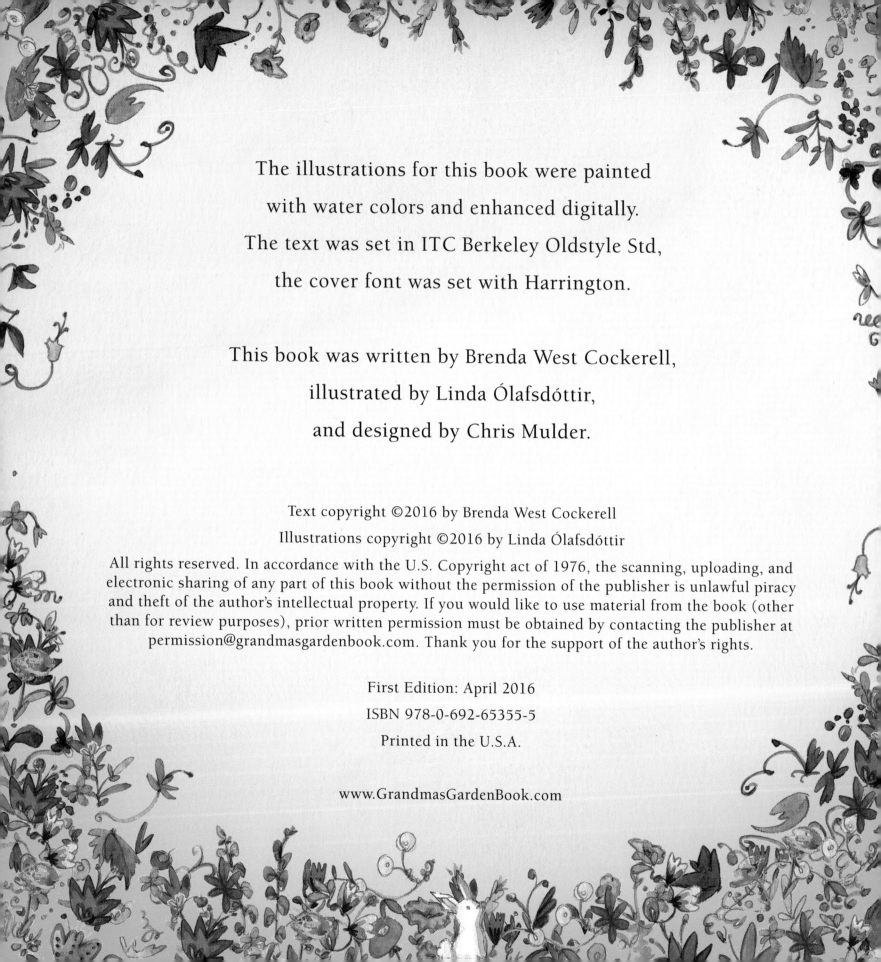

The illustrations for this book were painted
with water colors and enhanced digitally.
The text was set in ITC Berkeley Oldstyle Std,
the cover font was set with Harrington.

This book was written by Brenda West Cockerell,
illustrated by Linda Ólafsdóttir,
and designed by Chris Mulder.

First Edition: April 2016

ISBN 978-0-692-65355-5

Printed in the U.S.A.

www.GrandmasGardenBook.com